Horses
On The Farm

Joanne Mattern

ROURKE
PUBLISHING
www.rourkepublishing.com

www.rourkepublishing.com

PHOTO CREDITS: Title Page: © Matthew Dixon; Page 3: © Oleg Kutseruco; Page 5: © January Welsh; Page 7: © chelovek; Page 8: Maria Itina; Page 9: © Ina Van Hateren; Page 11: © Lars Christensen; Page 12: © Yulia Chupina; Page 13: ©Bill Dodge; Page 15: © Mikhail Kondrashov; Page 17: © Becky Hermanson; Page 18: © Nathan McClunie, © hypermania2; Page 19: © Margo Harrison; Page 20: © Elena Ioachim; Page 21: © Rick Carlson; Page 22: © Bonzami Emmanuekke; Back Ground: © Russ Lickteig

Edited by Precious McKenzie

Cover by Nicola Stratford, Blue Door Publishing
Interior design by Tara Raymo

Library of Congress Cataloging-in-Publication Data

Mattern, Joanne, 1963-
  Horses on the farm / Joanne Mattern.
      p. cm. -- (On the farm)
  Includes bibliographical references and index.
  ISBN 978-1-61590-266-8 (Hard Cover) (alk. paper)
  ISBN 978-1-61590-506-5 (Soft Cover)
  1. Horses--Juvenile literature. 2. Horse farms--Juvenile literature. I. Title.
  SF302.M2486 2011
  636.1--dc22
                        2010009854

Rourke Publishing
Printed in the United States of America, North Mankato, Minnesota
033010
033010LP

www.rourkepublishing.com - rourke@rourkepublishing.com
Post Office Box 643328 Vero Beach, Florida 32964

Table of Contents

Many Horses

There are almost 200 different **breeds** of horses. Horses come in different colors and sizes.

Many horses have white patches of fur on their bodies. These patches are called markings.

Blaze marking

Star and stripe marking

Star marking

Big and Small

Horses are measured in **hands**. A hand measures about four inches. Most horses stand sixteen hands high. That equals almost 64 inches tall (163 centimeters).

Horses are measured at the shoulder.

Not all horses are big. A **pony** measures less than 58 inches (147 centimeters).

If you want to get a horse, a Shetland pony is a good choice. They stay small even when they are fully grown.

A Horse's Food

Horses eat grass and other plants. When horses graze in fields, they pull up plants with their strong teeth.

Most horses eat 20 to 25 pounds (9 to 11 kilograms) of food each day.

On a farm, a horse also eats **oats** and other grains. They eat carrots and apples, too.

An apple is a tasty and healthy snack!

Life on the Farm

Many horses live on farms. They graze and run in the fields during the day. At night they go into the **stable** to sleep. In the stable each horse has its own **stall**.

Stall doors open at the top to let in light and air.

A Horse is Born

A female horse is called a **mare**. Mares give birth to a baby called a **foal**. A foal can stand up right after it is born.

Foals stay with their mothers for 3 to 12 months after they are born.

How Horses Help People

Horses help people in many ways. People like to ride horses. Some people ride horses in races or **competitions**.

Barrel Racing

Polo

In competition, some horses may jump obstacles up to 6.5 feet (2.0 meters) high.

Horses aren't just for riding! Farmers also harness horses to carts and wagons to pull heavy loads.

Horses also do work. Horses help on the farm. Cowboys ride horses to herd cattle.

Some horses are specially trained by cowboys to herd cows.

Horses make a farm a fun place to live!

Glossary

breeds (BREEDZ): types of animals

competitions (kom-puh-TISH-uhnz): contests

foal (fohl): a baby horse

hands (HANZ): a unit used to measure horses; about four inches

mare (mair): a female horse

oats (ohtz): a type of grass used as food

pony (POH-nee): a horse that stands less than 58 inches (147 centimeters) tall

stable (STAY-buhl): a building that houses horses or cattle

stall (STAWL): a section in a barn for one horse

Index

Websites to Visit

www.horsefun.com

www.kidsfarm.com/horses.htm

www.historyforkids.org/learn/environment/horses.htm

www.enchantedlearning.com/subjects/mammals/horse/Horsecoloring.shtml

About the Author

Joanne Mattern has written more than 300 books. She lives in New York state with her husband, four children, and an assortment of pets that includes cats, geckos, fish, and a turtle, but no horses.